SAINT CATHERINE OF SIENA

*"Blessed are the peacemakers: for they
shall be called the children of God."*
—Matthew 5:9

Saint Catherine of Siena

SAINT CATHERINE OF SIENA

1347-1380

By

F. A. Forbes

"Who shall find a valiant woman? Far and from the uttermost coasts is the price of her."
—Proverbs 31:10

TAN BOOKS AND PUBLISHERS, INC.
Rockford, Illinois 61105

Nihil Obstat: C. Schut, S.T.D.
Censor Deputatus

Imprimatur: Edmund Canon Surmont
Vicar General
Westminster
November 24, 1913

This book, the Second Edition, was formerly published in 1919 by R. & T. Washbourne, Ltd., London, as part of the series *Standard-bearers of the Faith: A Series of Lives of the Saints for Young and Old.*

ISBN 0-89555-622-7

Library of Congress Catalog Card No.: 98-61413

The illustrations by Franchi are frescoes by Alessandro Franchi in the Church of St. Catherine at Siena.

Cover illustration: The young St. Catherine cutting her hair in order to avoid betrothal. Fresco by Alessandro Franchi. Photo: B. N. Marconi, Genoa, Italy.

Printed and bound in the United States of America.

TAN BOOKS AND PUBLISHERS, INC.
P.O. Box 424
Rockford, Illinois 61105
1998

"Thanks be to the Highest God Eternal, who has placed us in the battlefield as knights to fight for His Bride with the shield of holiest faith."

—Letters of St. Catherine of Siena

St. Catherine of Siena praying for the soul of a criminal
about to be executed. (Detail from a painting by Sodoma,
1477-1549, in the Church of St. Dominic, Siena).

CONTENTS

Famous portrait of St. Catherine of Siena painted by
Andrea Vanni (1332-c.1414), one of Catherine's disciples.
(Portrait in the Church of St. Dominic, Siena).

SAINT CATHERINE OF SIENA

"She glorifieth her nobility by being conversant with God: yea and the Lord of all things hath loved her." —Wisdom 8:3

Chapter 1

THE SUNSHINE OF FONTEBRANDA

"By a certain excess of joy they took from her her proper name, calling her not Catherine, but Eufrosina, nor know I by what instinct." —*Fra Raimondo of Capua*

TOWARD the south of Tuscany, enthroned on her three hills, her quaint old towers soaring into the blue Italian sky, stands Siena, the city of the Virgin. Few of the cities of Italy have changed so little in the course of the centuries as she. The frowning walls of a medieval stronghold still surround her, broken here and there by great gates on whose brick arches the blue and crimson and gold of the fourteenth century painters yet linger. Her old palaces, her gorgeous cathedral, her noble churches, her steep and narrow streets have changed but little in the last six hundred years.

The very name of Siena seems to bring with it a fragrance of lilies. It is the city of the Virgin Mother of God, solemnly dedicated to her

1

in the year 1260, on the eve of the great battle of Montaperti, when the citizens of Siena
won a glorious victory over the rival republic of
Florence.

"Follow me now," cried the leader of the
Sienese army, fitly named Buonaguida, "let us
surrender ourselves, our city, with all our rights,
to the Queen of Eternal Life, to Our Lady and
Mother, the Virgin Mary. Follow me, all of you,
with purity of faith and freedom of will to make
this offering." Three days of thanksgiving followed on the victory, and for centuries after the
favorite subject of the painters of Siena was that
"Lady and Mother" who had helped their city
in her need.

Not quite a hundred years after the battle of
Montaperti, in the year 1347, there was born
to Jacomo Benincasa, a well-to-do dyer of Siena,
and his wife Lapa, a little daughter who was
destined to be the glory of her native city and
one of the most remarkable women of her time.
The child, who was the youngest of a large family of sisters and brothers, was christened Catherine; but the little maid was so sweet and lovable,
her winning ways and innocent baby talk had
such power to comfort and cheer those who were
sad or in trouble, that the neighbors called her
"Eufrosina" or "Joy." Monna Lapa would often
miss her little daughter and find that she had

been carried off by someone who was feeling lonely or sorrowful, and loud would be the outcries when the mother appeared to take possession of her baby. The sunshine that played round the golden head of the little Catherine seemed to have found its way into her heart, so happy was she, so innocently wise her childish sayings and so gentle the touch of her tiny hand.

It was a matter of course in Siena that every child should love the Blessed Virgin, but Catherine seems to have had a special devotion from her earliest babyhood to the Virgin Mother of God. As soon as she could speak she learned the Hail Mary, and she would kneel to say it on every step as her little feet climbed up the steep staircase of her father's house.

We are told that Monna Lapa, watching from the kitchen below, would often see the child carried from the top to the bottom of the stairs by the hands of Angels and would tremble lest she should fall. The things of Heaven seemed already as familiar to her as the things of earth, and she was not yet seven years old when she saw the first of those wonderful visions which were to become so frequent in later years.

"Blessed are the pure of heart," said Jesus Christ, "for they shall see God." They see Him indeed, even in this life, by faith and by love, the two eyes of the soul. But to some of His

Saints, whose one desire is to preserve that purity of heart in the midst of the corruptions of the world, He "who feedeth among the lilies" reveals Himself in a more close and intimate manner. The veil that hides the spiritual world from the world of sense is for a moment withdrawn and the creature is allowed to hear the sounds and see the sights of Paradise.

Visions and ecstasies are hard things to understand, but they ought not to be hard to believe. God is the same in all ages—yesterday, today and forever. He who showed Himself to Paul on the road to Damascus, and in vision after vision to St. John on the Isle of Patmos, can show Himself and has shown Himself to His servants even in these days of ours when faith and love are weak. Some people will not believe the things they cannot prove and test by human methods, but to others the fact that the mysteries of the Infinite God are beyond their finite understanding is the strongest proof of the faith they cherish.

The little Catherine had been sent one day with her brother Stephen to the house of their married sister Bonaventura. As the two children on their way home passed the fountain of Fontebranda, Catherine, who was looking up at the Church of St. Dominic which stands on the opposite hill, saw in the heavens the figure of

Our Lord robed and crowned pontifically. He stretched out His right hand and blessed her solemnly with a smile of surpassing sweetness. The child stood rooted to the ground, knowing nothing of what was passing around her, her eyes fixed on the beautiful vision, rapt in wonder and joy.

Stephen, missing her at his side, turned to look for her. "Catherine!" he cried, but the child seemed not to hear him. "Catherine, Catherine!" he repeated, running to his little sister and pulling her by the hand with all his strength, "what are you doing? Why do you look up like that?" At this the little girl seemed to come to herself. She burst into tears, for at his touch the vision had vanished. "Ah," she said, "if you had seen what I saw you would never have pulled me away," but she did not tell her brother what had happened. It was not till years afterwards, when it had become a habitual thing for her to see and converse with Our Lord, that she told her confessor of this early vision of her childhood.

After this first glimpse into Paradise, Catherine became more silent and thoughtful. She had seen the King in His beauty, and He had drawn her young heart to Him forever. A short time afterwards she made a vow to the Blessed Virgin to consecrate herself to God. "Here I give my faith and promise," said the child aloud, kneeling upon the floor with her hands clasped in prayer, "to Him and to thee that I will never take another spouse but Him, and so far as in me lies, will keep myself pure and unspotted for Him alone to the end of my days."

She longed to live the life of those holy hermits and Saints of whom she had so often heard and would creep away by herself to spend long hours in prayer. She would mortify her childish appetite by passing part of her portion at meals to her brother Stephen or slipping it under the table to the cats. She scourged herself with a little whip of cords.

Already, young as she was, we find the spirit of an apostle strong in her child heart. The Saints whom she loved the best were those who, not content with seeking their own perfection, spent their lives in drawing the souls of their fellowmen to God. Hearing that the great St. Dominic had founded an order expressly for this purpose, Catherine would follow the Dominican friars when they passed down the steep street and would kiss the place where they had set their feet. So sweetly would she speak of the things of God to her little playmates that they would leave their childish games to join her in her prayers, finding a greater happiness in her company.

When Catherine was twelve years old—and

in Italy in those days a girl was considered grown up at that age—her parents bade her take more pains to dress her beautiful hair becomingly, for they wished to find a husband for her and to settle her in a home of her own. In vain Catherine told them that she would never marry; they could not understand such a resolution and thought that she was moved by a childish obstinacy. They began to treat her harshly and unkindly, thinking that her refusal to obey them was due to her love of prayer. They took away from her her own little room and sent her to the kitchen to do the work of a servant, that she might never be alone or free to think of God.

But Catherine bore their harsh and cutting words with sweetness and gentleness. No longer having a moment to herself, she resolved to make a little cell in her own heart, where she might live in the presence of her Beloved. While she was hard at work in the kitchen she would think to herself that she was in the Holy House at Nazareth. Her father she pictured as Our Lord, and her mother as the Blessed Virgin; the rest of the household were the Apostles and disciples of Christ. "Because of this imagination," says Fra Raimondo of Capua, "she seemed to serve them all with such great gladness and diligence that every one marvelled."

To prove to her mother that she was earnest in her resolve, she cut off all her beautiful golden hair and wore a little cap upon her head, but this only angered Monna Lapa the more. Her daughter's hair, she angrily declared, would grow again, and in the end she would have to give in to her parents. Yet no unkindness could move the young girl from her gentle patience; and the wonderful sweetness with which she bore her trial began at last to make an impression on her father. He was a good man and had honestly thought at first that Catherine's refusal to marry was nothing but a childish whim. He now began to see that it was something more. Passing the door of Stephen's room one day, he saw Catherine kneeling on the floor in prayer, a white dove, which flew out of the window as he entered, hovering above her head.

"What dove was that?" he asked; but Catherine replied in astonishment, "Sir, I never saw or heard a dove in the chamber." Jacomo was greatly astonished, and he spoke to his wife of what he had seen.

At the same time Catherine's doubts as to the way in which God was calling her to serve Him were forever set at rest. One day as she was praying in her brother's room, the only spot now where she could be for a moment alone, St. Dominic appeared to her in a vision and promised her that she should one day wear the habit of his order.

The time had come to speak. Catherine told her family of the vow she had made to consecrate herself to God, and her determination to be faithful to it. For that reason she could not, she said, take an earthly husband, as her parents wished. If it pleased them to keep her at home as their servant, she would serve them willingly and obediently, but to Christ alone, her chosen Spouse, she would belong. Her gentle and modest words completely conquered her father, though Lapa still wept at the overthrow of all her hopes.

"Dearest daughter," said Jacomo, "God forbid that we should desire anything contrary to His Holy Will. In His Name, therefore, follow freely what you have vowed; from this day forth none in the house shall hinder you. Only pray for us to your Heavenly Spouse, that we may be found worthy of the eternal life which He has promised."

Chapter 2

THE PREPARATION

"Where shalt thou rejoice? Upon the Cross with the spotless Lamb, seeking His honor and the salvation of souls, through continual humble prayer." —*Letters of St. Catherine*

CATHERINE was now free to give herself up to the life to which she felt God was calling her. Under her father's house was a little cell, lighted by one small window, and here she took up her abode. A few bare planks formed her bed by night and a bench by day. A crucifix and a picture of Our Lady, before which she kept a lamp continually burning, hung upon the wall; save for these the room was empty. But in it, poor as it was, Catherine found the solitude and silence that her heart desired.

During three years, save to go to Mass at the Church of St. Dominic close by, she scarcely ever left her cell. It was to be to her the very gate of Heaven; in it was to begin that life of prayer and intimacy with God that was to last throughout her life, though later under such different circumstances.

She increased her penances, for she had learned that prayer, if it is to be fruitful, must go hand in hand with things which are hard to nature. She schooled herself to eat less and less until at last she managed to do almost entirely without food, and the hours that she spent in sleep on her bed of boards became gradually shorter and shorter. The iron chain that she bound round her tender body made every movement a pain, and she scourged herself several times a day until the blood flowed. All this is hard for us even to read about and harder still for us to understand unless we know the motive that urged her, as it has urged so many of the Saints, to such terrible austerities.

This Catherine tells us herself. "Thou shouldst not, my soul," she says, "thou that art a member, travel by another road than thy Head. An unfit thing it is that limbs should remain delicate beneath a thorn-crowned Head." That thorn-crowned Head bent continually toward her from the crucifix, and at the sight of the wounds that her Beloved had borne for her, Catherine, like all true lovers, longed to give Him "blood for blood."

Again, we must remember that closely bound up with that ardent love of Christ was the love of her fellowmen—those souls that she longed to draw to Him. All around her she saw men and women giving themselves up to sin and to contempt of their Creator, and this was another strong motive for penance. We know from her own words that for the salvation of others she was ready to bear the pains of Hell. "I am fain to offer Thee my body in sacrifice," she said one day to Our Lord, "and to bear all for the world's sins, that Thou mayst spare it, and change its life for another."

It was from Our Lord Himself that she learned the value of suffering. She was praying one day that she might be strong to resist evil and to fight against temptation.

"Daughter, embrace the Cross," said Our Lord to her, "and for My sake look on all sweet things as bitter, and all bitter things as sweet, and so be certain that you will always be strong."

When Catherine was about seventeen years old she was clothed with the habit of the Sisters of Penance of St. Dominic, the "Mantellate," as they were called in Siena. She received the white robe of purity and the black mantle of humility—in which the pictures of the Sienese painters have made her so familiar to us—in the little side chapel of the Church of St. Dominic, which is still fragrant with her memory and which was one of her favorite places of prayer.

Here it was that, asked one day for alms by

a poor beggar and having no money, she took the little silver cross from her rosary and gave it to him. The day after, she was again in the chapel when Our Lord appeared to her smiling, with the little cross, blazing with jewels, in His hand. "Daughter, knowest thou this cross?" He asked; "yesterday thou gavest it to Me with a great love and charity, and on the Day of Judgment I will show it in the presence of men and Angels."

In this chapel it was that Our Lord, again appearing to Catherine in a vision, opened her breast and put there His own Heart, saying "Lo, most dear daughter Mine, even as the other day I took from thee thy heart, so do I now give thee Mine own, by which thou shalt ever live." In this chapel is still shown the pillar against which Catherine used to lean in her ecstasies, and here it was that she received miraculous Communion at the hands of Our Lord Himself.

The Mantellate were not nuns, strictly speaking. They lived a good and holy life in their own homes, working among the poor and nursing the sick. They were for the most part elderly women or widows, and they had objected at first to receiving Catherine on account of her youth. After having seen her and spoken with her, however, they had been so much struck by her modesty and wisdom that they had consented to accept her.

It seemed to her now as if God had granted her all her heart's desire, and she gave herself up to continual prayer and communion with Our Lord in the little cell that was to her so full of His presence. Heaven was very close to Catherine in her purity and holiness, and the veils that hid the supernatural from the sensible world grew very thin. Sometimes she smelled the fragrance of the lilies of Paradise, and standing by night at her little window, it was given to her to hear the angelic songs of Heaven. Our Lord Himself continually appeared to her, and spoke to her familiarly as "friend to friend." She told her confessor that she could often hear the voices of the Saints singing in the eternal song of praise, and that those who had loved Our Lord the most on earth sang more strongly and sweetly than all the rest. One day she suddenly stopped speaking and seemed rapt in ecstasy. "Do you not hear, Father," she asked him, "with what a high sweet voice the blessed Magdalen sings in the choir of the Blessed?"

Although Catherine knew so much about the things of God, she had no more education than other girls of her class in the fourteenth century. She did not even know how to read, and this was a continual grief to her, for she had a great desire to be able to say the Divine Office and to study the Sacred Scriptures and other

The Divine Beggar

Painting: Alessandro Franchi

Photo: Alinari

The Night of the Nativity

holy books. She borrowed an alphabet from her sister and tried to teach herself, but it seemed to her a very difficult thing. Then she prayed to Our Lord and asked Him to be her Teacher, and after that all became easy.

When she was saying the daily Office, Our Lord would come to her in her little cell and walk up and down with her reciting the Psalms. Catherine told her confessor that when she came to the end of the Psalm they were reciting together, instead of saying, as it was written in the prayer book, "Glory be to the Father and to the Son," she would say, "Glory be to the Father and to *Thee*" and turn to our Blessed Lord as she spoke.

She loved to unite her prayers to those of her brothers, the Dominican friars. From her little cell she could hear the bell that called them to the church for Office. At night while they slept she remained in prayer; but at midnight, when she heard the bell of St. Dominic's ringing for matins, she would rise from her knees. "Lord," she would say, "until now my brethren have slept, and I have watched for them in Thy Presence. Now they are rising to offer Thee their praises; suffer me to take a little rest." Then she would lie down on her hard couch and sleep.

Thus, in the solitude of her little cell, her Divine Spouse was fashioning Catherine after

His own Heart to the work He had for her. The first lesson she was to learn was that of her own weakness and of His strength. "Knowest thou, My daughter," He said to her one day, "what thou art and what I am? I am He who is, and thou art that which is not." The second lesson was that of self-forgetfulness. "A soul that loves God perfectly," she told her confessor, "ends by forgetting herself and all other creatures."

But the fashioning was not ended. Catherine had yet to pass through the fires of temptation. The sweet visions ceased; Our Lord seemed to have forsaken her, while her cell was haunted by frightful figures who whispered evil thoughts in her ear and who pursued her even to the church with their hideous suggestions. "Why chastise your body thus?" they said, "you will never have courage to persevere. Life is for enjoyment, not for suffering. You will lose both the joys of this life and the happiness of the next; you will never endure to the end."

Then Catherine set herself to fight bravely and not to look for comfort, for she remembered Our Lord's words to her when she had prayed for strength: "If you suffer with Me, you will also be rewarded; accept all adversities with a willing and cheerful heart." But the evil spirits beset her more and more strongly. "You cannot resist us," they said; "we will give you no peace until you give in to us; we will make your whole life unbearable by our torments."

Then Catherine answered quietly, "I have chosen pain for my comfort; therefore, it will not be difficult for me to bear for the love of my Lord all that you shall do to me." At these words the evil spirits left her, and in the midst of a glorious light she saw Our Lord Himself standing before her. "Mine own daughter Catherine," He said, "I have suffered for thee; think it not much therefore to suffer for Me." But Catherine asked Him where He had been all the time when she had been beset by such horrible temptations.

"Daughter," He replied, "I was in your heart, taking great delight to see love and holy fear and faith so strong in it. The pains of My servants are no delight to Me, but I rejoice to see their readiness to suffer patiently and gladly for My sake. Now that you have so bravely fought your battle, I will be with you more closely and will visit you more often than before." Then Catherine was filled with a great joy and gladness, and all her pain was forgotten.

She had asked for purity and strength, and God had answered her prayer. "Give me now, O Lord," she prayed, "a more perfect faith, that nothing may ever separate me from Thee"; and Our Lord answered her, "I will espouse thee to

Myself in faith."

It was at the end of the Carnival time, and everybody in Siena was making merry and thinking only of amusement. Catherine knelt in her little cell praying, for she knew how many sins were being committed during those days of wild enjoyment.

Suddenly a great light shone in her little room and Our Lord appeared to her with the Blessed Virgin, St. John, St. Paul and St. Dominic. Our Blessed Lady took Catherine by the hand and, holding it out to her Divine Son, asked Him to espouse Catherine to Himself. He drew out a ring set with four glistening pearls and a diamond that shone like the sun, which He placed on the finger of Catherine's right hand, saying, "Behold, I have espoused thee to Me, thy Maker and Saviour." Then the vision vanished, but all her life long Catherine could see the ring of her Beloved upon her finger, the token that she belonged to Him forever.

Chapter 3

GOD'S WILL—GOD'S WAY

"What hast Thou taught me, O Love Uncreated? Thou hast taught me that I should bear patiently like a lamb, not only harsh words, but even blows harsh and hard, and injury and loss."　　　　*—Letters of St. Catherine*

THE solitude and the silence of the little cell beneath her father's house had grown so dear to Catherine that she would gladly have stayed in it for the rest of her life, but this was not God's will for her. She was destined for a great mission; hers was to be the work of an apostle, the winning of souls for Christ.

It was about this time that He made known to her His desire that she should begin to take part in the family life of the household and tend the poor and the sick in her own town of Siena. The life of prayer was not to cease, but it was to go hand in hand with action. It was a sacrifice to Catherine to give up the quiet life that she loved so much, but she had learned to renounce her own desires and to find her hap-

21

piness in the will of God.

The household of Jacomo Benincasa and his wife Lapa was a large and busy one. Several of the elder sisters and brothers were married and lived with their children in their father's house. Catherine could find plenty to do at home as well as abroad. Looking upon herself as the last and the least of all, she was always ready to do what was hardest, making herself the servant of everyone who was in need of help. Though constantly in pain, for the austerities she practiced had affected her health, she was always cheerful and merry, and the radiant happiness of her face impressed everyone who saw her. The sick and the poor were her especial care, and Jacomo allowed her to give freely from his little store to all who were in want.

Perhaps the greatest proof of true holiness is the patient bearing of injuries and affronts. It seems, says St. Ambrose, as if all who are called to a very close and intimate friendship with God have sooner or later to pass this test.

In one of the hospitals in the town lay a poor woman so terribly afflicted with leprosy that no one would attend to her. Catherine offered to be her nurse, and would go every day after hearing Mass at St. Dominic's to wash and dress her sores, make her bed and prepare her food. Monna Lapa, who was afraid that her daughter might

contract the terrible disease, begged her not to
run such a risk, but Catherine replied that what
she was doing she did for God, who would not
let her suffer in consequence.

The poor woman, who was at first grateful
for the tender care she received, soon began to
presume on the charity and humility of her nurse.
If Catherine were a moment late, she would
scold and abuse her as if she had been her slave,
and find fault with everything that she did.
"Have patience a moment, dear mother," Catherine would gently answer, "and I will do all as
you wish"; and the more her ungrateful patient
abused her, the more tenderly and lovingly did
she serve her. At last, as the disease increased in
violence, the terrible signs of it appeared on
Catherine's hands. Monna Lapa was loud in her
outcries, but her daughter, wholly forgetful of
herself, continued to tend the poor creature until
her death. Then, when she had prepared the
body for burial—for no one else would touch
it—her trust in God was justified and she was
miraculously healed.

This came to the ears of one of the Sisters
of Penance, an old woman called Palmerina who,
though she had given her wealth to the service
of God, was of a proud and envious disposition.
She could not bear to hear others praised and,
conceiving a great dislike for the gentle young

Sister of whom everybody spoke with admiration, never let pass an occasion of saying hard things about her.

It was a great distress to Catherine that she should be the cause of sin to another, and hearing that Palmerina was very ill and not expected to live, she went to her to see if she could not win her to a better frame of mind. Her efforts only seemed to increase the bitterness and the hatred in the old woman's heart, and after listening impatiently for a few moments, she cursed her visitor and bade her begone.

Then Catherine had recourse to prayer and for three days besought Our Lord that she, whose only desire was to bring souls to Him, might not be the cause of the loss of this one. Her prayers were heard. Palmerina sent for her and, after having asked her pardon for all that she had said against her, received the Last Sacraments and died in peace. After her death Our Lord made it known to Catherine that it was through her earnest prayers that this soul had been saved; and she, after thanking Him with deep humility, asked as a special grace that it might in the future be given to her to see the souls of those with whom she conversed, rather than their bodies. This gift God granted to her, as we shall see.

It was often from her own sisters in religion

and from good people that Catherine had the most to suffer. They could not understand the way in which God was leading her, and they sometimes distrusted her conduct. So great was her devotion to the Blessed Sacrament that after Communion she would often remain for several hours in an ecstasy, without moving or being conscious of anything around her. "Why could she not behave like other people," they asked, "and go home quietly after Mass? Who was Catherine Benincasa that she should set herself up as being a Saint?" They even induced the Dominican friars to change her confessor and to deprive her of Holy Communion. Catherine bore it all with her usual patience and humility, believing that they were really seeking the good of her soul. When she was told that some people looked on her as a hypocrite and a deceiver, she only answered that she was indeed the greatest of sinners and that she would like to kiss the feet of those who knew her so well.

A certain Franciscan of Pisa, Fra Lazzarino, had heard of Catherine's ecstasies and was convinced that she was an impostor. He did not conceal his opinion when talking with others, especially when he was sent to Siena to lecture on philosophy. Seeing, however, that the people would not believe him, he resolved to visit Catherine and try to make her commit herself in some

way. For this purpose he went to Fra Bartolommeo, a Dominican friar who was a friend
of Catherine's, and asked to be taken to her
house. Fra Bartolommeo, who felt sure of the
results of the interview, consented at once.

As soon as they were seated in her cell, Fra
Lazzarino remarked that he had heard so much
of Catherine's holiness that he had come to visit
her in order that her conversation might edify
and comfort his soul. To this Catherine replied
humbly that he, learned in the Scriptures and
an eloquent preacher, was much more fitted to
comfort her poor little soul than she was to help
him. This was not quite what he had expected,
and after a short time he rose to go, saying that
he would return another time. Then Catherine,
kneeling modestly before him, begged for his
blessing and his prayers, and he, more as a matter of form than because he desired it, asked her
to pray for him, to which she gladly consented.

During that night and all the next day the
Franciscan was beset by such a deep sense of
contrition that he could do nothing but shed
tears, and at last he began to ask himself in what
way he had offended God. A voice answered in
his heart, "Have you forgotten that last night,
although you were not in earnest, you asked My
servant Catherine to pray for you?" At this Fra
Lazzarino hastened to Catherine's house and,

falling at her feet, besought her to direct him in the way of God. Catherine begged him to rise and, at last, at his earnest entreaty, told him that it was God's will that he should practice more perfectly his vow of poverty, following his Lord in nakedness and humility. The Franciscan realized, as she spoke, how greatly he had been at fault on this point, and he determined to follow his rule more strictly. He became one of the holiest and humblest of the followers of St. Francis and a true friend to St. Catherine.

Her trials, however, were not yet ended. A woman called Andrea, who belonged to the Sisters of Penance, was dying of cancer, and so noisome was the disease that no one had courage to remain near her. Catherine, on hearing this, went with her usual charity to offer her services to the sick woman. Andrea was one of those people who had spoken strongly against Catherine and who were inclined to think that Catherine was a hypocrite. She accepted Catherine's charitable offer, as no one else could be found to assist her, but her mind was full of suspicious thoughts, and in spite of the unselfish love with which her young Sister served her, she denounced Catherine to the Prioress and Sisters of the Mantellate as a woman of bad life. It was a serious accusation, and Catherine was summoned to answer the charge.

Gently and humbly she replied to every question that she was innocent, but the lie told by Andrea grieved her sorely, and she prayed earnestly to Our Lord that He would Himself prove her innocence. In answer He showed her a crown of beautiful jewels and one of thorns and bade her choose between them. Catherine placed the crown of thorns upon her head. "Since Thou dost bid me choose," she answered, "I choose to be like Thee, and to bear crosses and thorns for Thy love as Thou hast done for love of me."

When the hard things that were being said about Catherine reached the ears of Monna Lapa, she, who was better able than anyone else to judge of the holiness of her daughter's life, was exceedingly angry. She told Catherine that if she went near Andrea again she would no longer look upon her as her child. Catherine was greatly troubled at this and, kneeling at her mother's feet, reminded her that Our Lord had bidden His children to love their enemies and do them good.

"If I should leave Andrea," she continued, "no one would take care of her, and so I should be the cause of her death. It is the devil who is deceiving her, but with God's grace she will know the truth and be sorry for what she has said."

Monna Lapa could never resist the pleading of her daughter, and Catherine returned to her

The Heavenly Espousals

29

The Crown of Jewels or The Crown of Thorns
(Fresco by Alessandro Franchi)

work of mercy. Her prayers and her charity at last prevailed. Andrea realized that she had been slandering a Saint, and she did all in her power to make reparation for her fault before she died.

The citizens of Siena were gradually becoming aware that there was one in their midst whose holiness made itself manifest to all who approached her, but there were still a few who could not or would not understand. Two friars, one a Franciscan and the other an Augustinian, thought that Catherine was an ignorant woman who was likely to lead others astray. Brother Gabriel, the Franciscan, who was a great theologian, lived, as unfortunately too many of his order were doing at the time, in a spacious cell, handsomely furnished, and surrounded with every luxury like a rich man.

The two, having determined to expose Catherine's ignorance, induced her confessor, Fra Tommaso della Fonte, to take them to see her, and they began at once to ask her the most difficult theological questions, hoping to put her to shame before several of her friends who were present. But God gave wisdom to His little servant, and with gentle humility she spoke to them in such wise of the love of Christ and of His service that they both began to realize how little they knew of either.

"Is there nobody here," cried Brother Gabriel

suddenly, "who will for the love of God go and give away everything that I have in my cell?" Henceforward he was faithful to the practice of poverty, and though he held a high position in his convent, he delighted to render the humblest services to his brethren. Both friars became friends and champions of the holy maiden whose burning words had made such an impression on their hearts.

When Catherine was twenty-one years old, Jacomo Benincasa died. He had been a good and tender father to Catherine, full of sympathy and understanding when she needed it the most, and though it was a deep grief to her to lose him, she rejoiced greatly at his readiness to go and at the holiness of his death. She it was who, during the sad days that followed, comforted and cheered her mother and the rest of the household, forgetting all grief in the joy of the knowledge given her by God that the soul of her father had passed from this earth straight to the glory of Heaven.

Chapter 4

THE DISCIPLES

"Not only her speech but also her whole being had a strange power, whereby the minds of men were in such wise drawn to good, and to delight in God, that all sadness was excluded from the hearts of those who conversed with her." —*Fra Raimondo of Capua*

IF Catherine had enemies, she also had many friends. It was not only her holiness that drew men and women of all classes to seek the company of the poor dyer's daughter of Siena, although there are few things so attractive as sanctity. God had given her a wonderful eloquence and power to read the inmost hearts of those with whom she came in contact. There was something so winning about Catherine's personality that few could resist her. At the same time, the simple wisdom with which, untaught as she was, she could converse with the most learned men convinced them that God Himself was her Teacher.

Her tender and loving heart, full of affection

and sympathy for those who were in distress, was open to all God's creatures. In the ordinary matters of daily life she showed a homely common sense that astonished, no less than did her keen and merry sense of humor, those who expected to find in her nothing but an unpractical mystic lost in dreams and visions. Great as was her horror of sin, she was never known to shrink from the vilest sinners while there was any hope of winning them to better things. She saw the possibilities that lay hidden under the most unpromising exterior, and it was her unwavering belief in the existence of that "better self" in human nature, however fallen, that so often gave people strength and courage to overcome the "worse."

During the time that she had been working among the sick and the poor in Siena, a little group of disciples had gathered round her, forming a spiritual family of which Catherine, young as she was, was not only the mother, but the very life and soul. Among these were several of the Mantellate or Dominican Sisters of Penance such as Alessia Saraceni, a young widow of noble birth who, in the early days of her friendship with Catherine, had given away all that she possessed to the poor, to serve Our Lord in poverty and penance. Lisa Colombini, Catherine's sister-in-law, who at her husband's death also became a Sister of Penance, and Francesca Gori, or "Cecca," were among the most faithful of her female companions.

There were also several Dominican friars who associated themselves with Catherine and looked to her for spiritual guidance, such as Fra Tommaso della Fonte, her first confessor; Fra Bartolommeo Domenico; Fra Antonio Caffarini, a learned man, who helped her in her study of the Scriptures; and Fra Raimondo of Capua, her third confessor and faithful friend, who became after her death Master General of the Dominicans and who wrote the famous *Legenda* or life of the Saint.

Then there was Messer Matteo, rector of the great hospital called the Misericordia, where Catherine and her sisters often worked; and Andrea Vanni the painter, politician as well as artist, whose portrait of the Saint, painted from life, still hangs in the Church of St. Dominic.

Some whom Catherine had rescued from a life of sin, such as Francesco de Malevolti, a young nobleman of Siena, also joined the spiritual fellowship and gave themselves to the service of God. He was twenty-five years old when he was first introduced to her, "not a little fiery and daring," as he himself tells us, and leading a selfish and worldly life. Catherine read his heart and revealed to him his miserable condition, with the result that he determined to amend. But it takes time to overcome bad habits, and the change did not come in a day, as we gather from a letter of Catherine's written later from Avignon: "With the desire of finding thee again, my little lost sheep, and putting thee back into the fold with thy companions. . . . Come, dearest son, I can well call thee dear, so much art thou costing me in tears and labors, and in much bitter sorrow."

It is good to know that the letter had its desired effect and that Francesco took fresh courage for the fight and triumphed gloriously in the end. During Catherine's life he frequently acted as her secretary and, after her death, having lost his wife and children, entered a monastery and died a holy death.

Perhaps the most interesting among the members of the "spiritual family" were three young Tuscan noblemen who attached themselves to the person of Catherine, dedicated their time and powers to her service and caught the fire of her noble ideals.

Neri di Landoccio, a young poet of Siena, was the first of the three to make her acquaintance. He was of a nervous and sensitive temperament and, like many other poets, subject to strange fits of sadness and despondency which, in spite of his great gifts, might have wrecked his life had not Catherine's strong spirit upheld him in his darkest moments.

Stefano Maconi was the second of the group. Young, gallant and well educated, his frank and joyous temperament made him a great contrast to Neri, who was his devoted friend. Catherine loved him for his innocence of life and saw all the possibilities of holiness that lay in his gay and joyous character. She trusted him above all her spiritual sons, and in her absence all looked to him as the head of the little family. After Catherine's death he became a Carthusian, and later on, General of the Order.

The circumstances of their first meeting are typical of Italy in the Middle Ages. One of the most powerful families in Siena, the Tolomei, had a deadly feud with the Maconi and their friends, and there were frequent fights between them. Stefano, sensible enough to deplore such a state of affairs, was advised by a friend to have recourse to Catherine, who had already acted as peacemaker in several such cases.

Catherine bade the members of both families meet her in the Church of San Cristoforo in the Piazza Tolomei, but when the day arrived, the Maconi and their friends were the only ones who chose to keep the appointment. Then Catherine knelt down before the high altar. "They will not listen to me," she said, "but they will have to listen to God."

Now it came to pass shortly afterward that the Tolomei and their friends, being close to the church, felt themselves impelled by a mysterious force to enter, and passing through the open door they found Catherine kneeling in ecstasy, surrounded by a strange and radiant light. Their hearts were softened at the sight, and then and there, before the altar, laying aside their hatred, they made peace with their foes. From that moment Stefano Maconi became Catherine's devoted friend.

The third of the little group was Barduccio Carrigiani, who joined Catherine later in life and was greatly beloved by her on account of his purity of heart. He was with her in Rome when she died and only survived her a short time. "Whilst he was at his last breath," writes Fra Raimondo, "he began to laugh, and so with a laugh of joy he gave up the ghost, in such wise that the signs of that joyous laugh still appeared in his dead body. This thing, I think, befell because in his passing he beheld her whom in life he had loved with true charity of heart, robed in splendor, coming with gladness to meet him."

There were monks and hermits too who visited the family from time to time and counted themselves among the number of Catherine's spiritual children. Not far from Siena was Lecceto, or the "Hermitage of the Woods." There lived William Flete, an Englishman from the University of Cambridge, and Giovanni Tantucci, better known as "John of the Cells," and a dear old hermit called Fra Santi, gentle and holy, who in his old age left the quiet of his cell to follow Catherine and work among the poor.

Last, but not least, there was Catherine's mother, good Monna Lapa, who also, after her husband's death, put on the habit of the Mantellate. She was known in the family as "Nonna" or "Granny" and lived to a great old age. A woman of the people, practical and sensible, she was not very spiritual, and she sometimes found it hard to understand the ways of her saintly daughter, for whom she nevertheless had the deepest reverence and affection.

To love Catherine was, for all who approached her, to draw near to God. The love of the disciples for their spiritual mother was, as one of them expressed it, "kindled at the foot of the Cross and consecrated on the steps of the altar." They looked to her for strength and support, and she never failed them. To her each one was a gift from God's own hand, and she never rested until she had drawn out the best that each had to give. "O sweetest Love," she prayed to her Divine Spouse, "let not the enemy snatch any one of them from my hands, but may all attain to Thee, O Eternal Father, to Thee Who art their final end."

The state of things in Siena in the fourteenth century was in no way different from that of the other Italian republics. The nobles were always fighting among themselves or with the *popolani* (people) for the ruling power, and changes of government were frequent. The state prisons were filled with men who, justly or unjustly, were accused of treason and condemned to bear the penalty. Catherine had a special tenderness for criminals and would visit them in their dungeons. Even when they were condemned to death, she would go with them to the place of execution.

Once when two poor wretches were passing the house where she was staying on their way to the scaffold, Alessia, hearing their blasphemies and screams of anguish—for they were being tortured as they went—called to Catherine. "O mother," she cried, "if ever you will see a pitiful sight, come now!" Catherine gave one look, and began to pray for the souls of the two poor criminals: "Remember the thief on the Cross, on whom Thou didst have mercy. Look down upon these wretched creatures, soften their hearts with the fire of Thy Holy Spirit, that they may be delivered from the second death."

Our Lord heard Catherine's prayers, and when the thieves, still blaspheming, reached the gate of the city, He appeared to them, showing His precious Wounds streaming with the blood that had been shed for their salvation and assuring them of forgiveness if they repented of their sins. To the wonder of all who were present, the two men cried out for a priest and, having with deep sorrow of heart confessed themselves, went to their death in great peace and comfort.

Many were the souls Catherine saved for her Divine Master in this way, but the most wonderful of all the conversions she effected was that of a young Perugian nobleman, Niccolo di Toldi, who had been sentenced to death for a hasty word spoken against the state. He had never practiced his religion, never even made his First Communion. When the priest, who was a friend of Catherine's, went to prepare him for death, the priest found him half mad with rage and despair and could do nothing with him.

Catherine, hearing of what had passed, went at once to the prison. The poor young man, hardly more than a boy in years, was touched at once by her gentle words and clung to her as a child clings to its mother. She stayed with him, comforting and soothing him till he was ready for Confession. When she left the prison, Catherine promised to come again the next day and go with him to the place of execution.

At break of day she returned, went to Mass with the poor prisoner and knelt beside him while he received Holy Communion for the first time in his life. "Take courage, my brother," she said, "for you are going to die washed in the adorable Blood of Jesus and with His sweet name on your lips." At this Niccolo was filled with strength and consolation so that he no longer feared to die; but Catherine went with him to the place of execution and, kneeling beside him, made the Sign of the Cross on his brow. There she remained, bending over him and speaking to him of God and of the life to come until the knife fell, when she received his head in her hands.

Standing thus in ecstasy, with the blood of the young man flowing over her white robe, Catherine had a vision of his soul as it entered Heaven turning to her in the joy of that new birth with a radiant look of farewell. "And all who were present," says he who wrote the account of it, "watching that strange scene in a deep hush of devotion, felt as if they were assisting at the death of a martyr rather than that of a criminal."

Chapter 5

IN GOD'S VINEYARD

"To the servant of God, every place is the right place, and every time is the right time.
—*Letters of St. Catherine*

IN the year 1374 the plague broke out in Siena. This terrible disease, known in England as the Black Death, had made its first appearance in Europe the year after Catherine's birth and swept over the whole of Italy, causing frightful mortality. Men and women were suddenly attacked while speaking to each other in the streets and died before they could reach their homes. The death carts went from door to door gathering up the dead, who were buried in great trenches outside the town. The richer citizens hastened to the country to escape the infection, but in many cases the disease followed them. The inmates of the plague-stricken houses fled in terror, leaving the sick to die untended. Bands of thieves, breaking into the rooms where the dead and the dying lay, carried off all the rich garments and jewels that they could lay hands

43

on and sold their plunder in neighboring cities and provinces, thus spreading the infection far and wide.

Two of Catherine's brothers, her sister Lisa and several of the little grandchildren that Monna Lapa was bringing up in her own house took the infection and died. Catherine tended them all and prepared the bodies for burial with her own hands. She wept over the little nephews and nieces that God had taken in the flower of their innocence, saying, to comfort her sad heart, "These, at least, I shall not lose."

Then, with a little band of devoted companions—Alessia, Cecca and the rest—she went forth into the most infected parts of the city, going from house to house, succoring the living and burying the dead.

In the places where the pestilence was raging most hotly these brave women would meet with another devoted little army—Fra Raimondo and his friars, who had vowed to lay down their lives, if need be, for their people. Day and night they labored in the hospitals and infected houses, carrying the succors of religion to the sick and the dying.

Many of these noble workers lost their lives. The rector of the great hospital of la Scala was stricken down at his post. Those who were carrying the dead to burial more than once fell lifeless and were buried in the still open grave. Messer Matteo, the rector of the Misericordia, while watching by a plague-stricken patient, was attacked himself by the terrible symptoms and sent for Fra Raimondo to make his last Confession. But Catherine, who knew the virtue of Messer Matteo and loved him much, hastened to the hospital.

"Rise up at once, Messer Matteo!" she cried, as she entered the room where the sick man lay, "this is not the time to be lying in bed"; and at her words the sickness left him, and he who had been at the point of death rose up hale and strong and went back to his work in the hospital. Another friend of Catherine's, the old hermit Fra Santi, also contracted the disease and was cured by her prayers.

Even Fra Raimondo did not escape. Feeling himself attacked by the plague as he was hastening through the city, he dragged himself with difficulty to Catherine's house, only to hear that she was absent. They sent for her in great haste. Laying her hand on the brow of the sick man, who was in great suffering, she knelt down beside him and fell into an ecstasy. As she prayed, the good friar felt the life returning to his aching limbs; and Catherine, coming to herself again, prepared food for him and bade him sleep. When he awoke he was perfectly well. "Go now," she said, "and work for the salvation of souls, and give thanks to Almighty God, who has preserved your life."

Famine and disorders of all kinds followed in the footsteps of the pestilence. During the time of scarcity Catherine multiplied bread to feed the poor many times by her prayers, as several of her contemporaries bear witness.

But the time of her great mission was drawing nigh. The country was in a sad condition. "Where is peace, where is liberty, where is tranquillity in Italy?" wrote a poet of the time. The Italian cities were either ruled by tyrants or, if republics such as Florence and Siena, were torn by internal quarrels and continually at war with their neighbors. Companies of foreign soldiers, ready to sell their swords to anyone who would pay them to fight, wandered through the country plundering and laying waste the land, unless bought off by the trembling citizens with large sums of money. Since the papacy of Clement V, the Popes had been at Avignon; and Italy, bereaved of her rightful protector, bewailed her desolation.

The greatest writers of the time express the feeling of sorrow that prevailed. Dante, in the year 1314, had written a letter to the Cardinals at Avignon demanding the return of the Popes to Rome. "You, the chiefs of the Church Militant," he writes, "have neglected to guide the chariot of the Bride of the Crucified One . . . you, who have been the authors of this confusion, must go forth manfully with one heart and one soul into the fray in defense of the Bride of Christ whose seat is in Rome, of Italy, in short of the whole band of pilgrims on earth." To Rome the establishment of the Popes in Avignon was disastrous. The city was left to anarchy and misery, and many of its beautiful churches and buildings were falling into ruins.

In 1370, three years before the outbreak of the plague in Italy, Gregory XI had succeeded Urban V on the papal throne. Gentle, scholarly and well-meaning, he was sickly in health and weak and irresolute in character. He was a Frenchman, and his love for his country and his own people scarcely seemed to point to a return to Rome.

Catherine, true patriot and lover of the Church as she was, deeply deplored the state of affairs in Italy and with prayers and tears besought her Divine Spouse to put an end to the evils that were harassing the country. Then God made it known to her that she, a poor weak daughter of the people, was to act as His instrument— not in her own power, but in lowliness of spirit, in utter trust of Him, a true reformer of the Bride of Christ. To her, the maiden image of

the Italian people, it was to be given to recon-
cile the Pope with Italy and to bring him back
to Rome.

Catherine's was indeed the spirit of the true
reformer—regeneration, not destruction, was her
dream. To her the Pope, whether Gregory or
Urban, was the representative of God—"Sweet
Christ on earth," as she loved to call him. Clear
of vision and strong in faith, she could look past
the faults and weaknesses of human nature and
see the thing signified behind the imperfect
earthly form. She could denounce with unflinch-
ing honesty the corruptions of the time, but the
Church of God was to her always the Mystical
Body of Christ, the Bride of the Crucified, outside of which was neither light nor peace.

She was already in correspondence with the
Pope, urging him to remedy the existing evils,
to be ready to give his life for Christ's flock and
to act manfully, appointing only worthy men to
rule the Church—above all, to return to Rome.
Her stirring appeal to all that was noblest and
best in Gregory's nature, her gentle deference,
the tender affection with which she wrote, now
as a daughter to a beloved father, now as a
mother to her son, would not fail in its effect.
The fame of Catherine's holiness and the wisdom which brought men of all ranks, politicians
as well as churchmen, to seek her counsel, had

already reached the ears of the Pope. He sent word to Siena that everything possible was to be done to help her in her work for souls, and he even dispatched one of his vicars to Siena to take her his apostolic benediction and to ask her prayers.

It was about this time that Catherine received an invitation from the ruler of the republic of Pisa to visit that city, and she set out accompanied by Monna Lisa, Alessia, Cecca and several Dominican friars, Fra Raimondo among the number. The Pisans received her as a messenger from God; her very presence seemed to draw men from sin to sanctity. So great was the reverence shown to her that some people were scandalized and others alarmed, lest she might be tempted to vainglory. One good man even took upon himself in all sincerity to warn her not to seek earthly praise or desire it. Catherine answered that she was deeply grateful for his care for her welfare and that she also often feared her own frailty and the deceits of the wicked one: "But I put my trust in the goodness of God," she continued, "and mistrust myself, for I know that on myself I cannot rely. I cling to the Holy Cross of Christ Crucified, and thereto I would be fastened."

This desire was to be indeed fulfilled in a strange and supernatural way. Close to the house where Catherine lodged in Pisa was the little Church of Sta. Cristina, where she often went to pray and which was to be associated ever afterwards with one of the most wonderful events in her spiritual life. On Laetare Sunday, as she was rapt in ecstasy after Holy Communion, Fra Raimondo and the others who were present saw her rise suddenly and stretch out both her arms, her face shining with an unearthly light. After a few moments she fell to the ground in a swoon. Alessia and Cecca, who were close behind her, caught her in their arms and carried her back to her room in an unconscious condition.

Later on Catherine told Fra Raimondo what had happened. She had seen, she said, the Crucified Lord coming down to her in a great light, while from His most Sacred Wounds five blood-red rays came down upon her feet and hands and heart, piercing them through and through. Though Catherine in her humility prayed that the sacred stigmata that she had thus received might be invisible during her life, after her death the marks of the Sacred Wounds were clearly visible on her body and were seen by several witnesses.

Pope Gregory in the early days of his pontificate had thought of a plan to put an end to the continual fighting between state and state in Italy. This was to unite all the princes and rulers of Christendom in a Crusade against the infidels. This project he had confided to Catherine, to whom strangely enough the same idea had occurred and who determined to use all her influence to bring it about. In this way the Free Companies of foreign soldiers could be gotten rid of, their love of fighting could be used for a good object and the country delivered from one of its worst evils. "Raise the Gonfalon of the most Holy Cross," she wrote to the Pope, "for with the fragrance of the Cross you shall win peace."

She herself, at Pisa, was doing all she could to stir up enthusiasm for the holy war, both by word of mouth and by her correspondence. Among the sovereigns and rulers whom she addressed was Joanna, the beautiful and wicked Queen of Naples, urging her in burning words to repent of her sins and to amend her life. "For Love's sake," she writes, "lift up the standard of the most Holy Cross in your heart . . . in all that is possible show yourself a faithful daughter of sweet and holy Church."

To several of the commanders of the Free Companies she also wrote—among others, to the famous English freelance Sir John Hawkwood: "With desire to see you a true knight and son of Jesus Christ. Now my soul desires that you should change your way of life and take the pay and the Cross of Christ Crucified, you and all your followers and companions, so that you may be Christ's Company . . . and thus you shall show that you are a true and manly knight."

It is good to know that the letter touched the vein of chivalry that was latent in the famous "soldier of fortune," wild and lawless though he was, and that he and his captains took a solemn oath on the Blessed Sacrament "and signed it with their hands and sealed it with their seal" to join the Crusade if it were started, and that Sir John even made a vow to join henceforward only in lawful warfare. Joanna of Naples too was touched by Catherine's appeal to her better nature and promised her assistance. But the project so nobly urged was never realized. During the dark days that followed, the Pope had other affairs to attend to. The hour for the Crusade was past.

Chapter 6

THE MISSION

"I shall give thee such speech and wisdom that no one shall be able to resist. I shall bring thee before Pontiffs and the rulers of the Church."
—*Words of Our Lord to St. Catherine*

CATHERINE was greeted by sad news when she returned to Siena. Not only had Bernabo Visconti, the Duke of Milan, one of the most violent and treacherous men of his time, stirred up the whole north of Italy to rebellion against the Pope, but the Republic of Florence had joined the League and was trying to induce the other cities of Italy to follow her example.

The Papal States had certainly had much to suffer. Gregory had appointed as his legates men without honor or humanity, who thought of nothing but their own advancement and whose cruel and unjust government had made the Pope, a stranger and a Frenchman whom the Italians had never even seen, exceedingly unpopular. To Catherine it seemed as if the powers of Hell were let loose against the Church. She realized and deplored the evils that had roused the anger of the people, but rebellion against the Pope was to her the most fearful evil of all.

Gregory determined to take strong measures. He placed Florence under an interdict. The churches were closed, priests were forbidden to administer the Sacraments and other towns and nations were forbidden to trade with the city. An army of hired soldiers under the leadership of Cardinal Robert of Geneva, a man of brilliant attainments but evil life, was sent to reconquer the Papal States.

To Catherine, whose whole desire was for peace, this was a double grief. She wrote a letter to Gregory beseeching him to overcome violence with gentleness and pointing out to him how greatly the behavior of the Legates had been to blame. Let him do away with these evil rulers and appoint good pastors and governors. "I pray you, in the name of Christ Crucified," she writes, "conquer their malice with your benignity. Do not look at the ignorance and pride of your sons; but with love and kindness, giving that gentle punishment and benign rebuke that will please your Holiness, render peace to us wretched children who have offended. I tell you, sweet Christ on earth, in the name of Christ in Heaven, that if you act thus they will all come in sorrow and lay their heads in your lap."

During these days of anguish Catherine had a vision in which her Divine Lord appeared to her and, placing the Cross upon her shoulder and the olive branch in her hand, bade her make peace in His Name. She had already written to the rulers of Florence a letter of strong reproach; she now wrote again offering herself as mediator between them and the Pope. "He who rebels against the Church is a rotten member," she writes, "and what is done to His Vicar on earth, be it reverence or insult, is done to God in Heaven. Think not that God is sleeping over the injuries that have been done to His Spouse . . . If through me anything can be done to unite you with Holy Church . . . I am ready to give my life."

Florence was already suffering severely from the interdict. The rulers knew something of Catherine's influence with the Pope, and her offer was at once accepted. Soon after Easter, accompanied by her little band of disciples, she set out for the rebellious city. She was received with every mark of honor, and her proposals were listened to with deference. The governors assured her that they were ready to throw themselves upon the Pope's mercy and submit themselves to him with all humility; for under these conditions alone, said Catherine, would she undertake to plead their cause. Ambassadors were to follow her shortly who were to be guided in all things by her advice.

At the end of May the little party set out for Avignon, riding through the lovely country of the Riviera washed by the blue waters of the Mediterranean, flooded in the early summer sunshine and carpeted with wild flowers. On the 18th of June they reached the beautiful city of Avignon, called on account of its chiming bells *la ville sonnante*.

It was not many years since Petrarch had written: "There is no piety there, no faith, no reverence for God, not any fear of Him, nothing holy, nothing just, nothing worthy of man." And another writer of the time, describing the evils in the Church, says: "The gold which is the holiness of virtues has grown dim in the Church, for all covet material gold. Ordinations and Sacraments are bought and sold for gold." But the veils that covered the fearful reality were fair enough. Gay courtiers and beautiful ladies paraded the streets of the city, which was the home of every art as well as of every vice; and amusement and enjoyment seemed the only end in life.

Among the splendid retinues of the Cardinals and courtiers, the crowds of magnificent prelates, gorgeously attired servants, minstrels, court ladies, actors and singers, a slender figure in white robe and black mantle threaded its way quietly and unnoticed. Yet, at the word of that humble ambassadress, the splendor and the renown of that "Babylon of the West" were to crumble forever into the dust of the past.

The Pope had provided a fine house with a beautifully decorated chapel for the use of Catherine and her friends. Soon after her arrival she was called to the papal presence. What were the thoughts of Gregory as he found himself for the first time face to face with the *Beata Popolana* of Siena—that maiden of the people whose strong mind and pure heart had such a strange power over the hearts and minds of the men of her time? We know only that before the interview was ended the Pope was so much impressed by Catherine, although she knew no French and had to make use of Fra Raimondo as interpreter, that he entrusted her with the whole management of the Florentine treaty, only bidding her "be careful of the honor of the Church."

Catherine lost no time in writing the good news to Florence. The ambassadors were daily expected; but days and weeks went by, and still they did not come. Catherine saw the Pope frequently, and she told him that she could not understand the delay. "Believe me, Catherine," he said, "they are deceiving you; they will not send, and if they do, it will come to nothing."

He was not far wrong. The Florentines were preparing to continue the war, although to save appearances they at last dispatched three ambassadors to Avignon. Catherine sent them a message to come to her, as the Pope had given her charge of their business. They replied rudely that they had received no instructions to confer with her; they had come to treat with the Pope. In spite of the contemptuous way in which she had been treated, Catherine continued to urge Gregory to indulgence, but as the Florentines had no intention of submitting, the embassy came to nothing, and the three returned to Italy.

But Catherine had a greater mission than that of making peace for Florence. She had never ceased since her arrival in Avignon to impress upon Gregory the necessity for his return to Rome. She reproached him greatly with the vices that reigned in the papal court, and besought him to choose his Cardinals and prelates more for their holiness of life than for their birth and rank.

People began to suspect what might be the result of her long conferences with the Pope and the influence that she was gaining over him. The French Cardinals dreaded above all things a return to Rome. It was greatly in the interests of France to keep the Pope in the country, and the great ladies of Avignon were by no means pleased at the idea of losing the splendor and the gaiety of the papal court. Some of these ladies came to visit Catherine, hoping to bring her round to their way of thinking.

For this purpose they pretended to be holy and pious, and they talked so eloquently about God that even Fra Raimondo was sometimes taken in. Not so Catherine, who read their very souls. She, always full of compassion and tenderness for the greatest of sinners, knew that she could do nothing here and would sit silent in their presence with her veil drawn over her face, or if she spoke at all, would say sadly: "First let us purify ourselves from our sins and escape from the bondage of Satan, and then we can talk about God."

The Countess of Valentinois, the Pope's sister, was a good woman and a true friend to Catherine. Desiring greatly to see her in ecstasy, she asked Fra Raimondo to let her come to the chapel one morning for Mass. She brought with her Elys de Turenne, the selfish and worldly young wife of the Pope's nephew, who was quite sure that the ecstasies were only a pretense and was determined to expose the fraud. She had armed herself with a long pin or sharp instrument of some kind and, bending down as if to kiss the border of Catherine's white robe, drove it several times with all her strength into her foot. Catherine felt nothing at the time; but later, when she came to herself, she was in great pain from the wounds, and could not walk for several days afterward.

The pleasure-loving, worldly-minded citizens of Avignon had reason for their fears. The inspiring influence of Catherine was calling out all that was best in Gregory, notwithstanding the efforts of the French Cardinals. He believed, in spite of his great love for his country and his own people, that it was his duty to return to Rome, and he had even in the early days of his pontificate made a vow to do so. When Catherine one day reminded him of this vow, of which no living creature knew but himself, he recognized more strongly than ever that the inspiration of God was directing His servant.

It was a hard fight. Italy was to him a strange country, torn with warfare, beset with dangers; and Gregory, though well meaning, was timid and too sensitive to the opinion of others. The Cardinals and the rest of his advisers did their best to paint the blackest possible picture of the probable results if he left France.

In order to escape their solicitations and those of his own family, which she knew Gregory was not strong enough to resist, Catherine bade him make his preparations in secret and announce his intention only when all was ready for the departure. At his request she put off her return to Italy so that she might remain near him to the end, and it was well that she did so.

A letter, supposed to have been written by a holy friar in Italy who was reported to have a gift of prophecy, was placed in Gregory's hands. In it he was warned that a plot had been made to poison him if he returned to Rome and that he would do better, if he had any such idea, to remain, at least for the time, at Avignon. The Pope took alarm at once and sent the letter to Catherine, who made short work of it.

"It seems to me a forgery," she writes, "and the hand that forged it is not a very skillful one; he ought to be sent back to school, for he writes like a child . . . I admire the words of this poisonous person who begins by advising good and holy actions and then desires you to give them up out of a fear for your bodily safety . . . That is not the language of the servants of God . . . He is administering the worst of all poisons, he is trying to prevent you from doing that which God demands of you . . . I pray you on behalf of Christ Crucified that you be no longer a timorous child, but manly. Open your mouth and swallow down the bitter for the sake of the sweet. Pardon me, Father, my over-presumptuous speech. Humbly I ask you to pardon me and give me your benediction."

The work was done. On September 15, 1376, Gregory left forever the papal palace at Avignon amid the tears and lamentations of the people. His old father, Count Guillaume de Beaufort, threw himself down on the threshold declaring that his son would leave the place only over his body. But it was the hour of Gregory's strength; his duty lay clear before him, and he passed stead-fastly on his way—a way beset with difficulties.

Through many storms the papal fleet made its way to Genoa where Catherine was waiting, having gone by another road. The Cardinals had declared that all the mishaps that had befallen them on the way were meant by God to turn the Pope from his purpose, and Gregory was wavering again. In the evening he went to the house where Catherine was staying to draw fresh strength and courage for the task that lay before him. He set sail soon after for Rome, where he was received by the citizens with every demon-stration of enthusiasm and joy.

After a long stay at Genoa occasioned by the serious illness of Neri and Stefano, Catherine went back to Siena, where Monna Lapa was impatiently awaiting her return. Catherine had fulfilled her mission, but the clouds were gath-ering more thickly than ever about the Church of Christ.

Chapter 7

THE PEACEMAKER

> "I have no other desire in this life save to
> see the honor of God, your peace, and the
> reformation of Holy Church, and to see the
> life of grace in every creature that hath rea-
> son in itself."
>
> —*Letters of St. Catherine of Siena*

THE two most powerful families in Siena were the Tolomei and the Salimbeni, who were continually at war with each other. Catherine, having many friends among them both, had done her best to make peace between them; but the governors of Siena, who hoped that the two families while quarreling with each other would have no leisure to fight with them, did all that they could to keep up the feud.

A fresh dispute now threatened to divide the Salimbeni. The head of the family died, and his young son Agnolino, wishing to be on peaceful terms with the republic, caused himself to be enrolled among the plebeian families of Siena and declared himself ready to support the cause of the people. Cione Salimbeni, Agnolino's quarrelsome and ambitious kinsman, jealous at the popularity which the young man had won by this proceeding, hastened to pick a quarrel with him, and civil war seemed likely to end the dispute. Countess Bianchina, the mother of Agnolino, and Stricca, the wife of Cione, were both devoted friends of Catherine, and it was to her that they turned in their distress. Their great castles lay ten miles apart among rocks and mountains, in a wild and savage country peopled only by chieftains who spent their lives in fighting and whose soldiers were little better than bands of robbers.

Catherine went first to Castiglioncella, the stronghold of Cione, who received her cordially and, although he had refused to listen to anyone else, consented at her request to give up the quarrel.

Agnolino was reported to be equally obstinate, but Catherine's first success had made her hopeful. She set out at once for the great castle of Rocca d'Orcia, where he was living.

To the men who dwelt in that wild region, prayer and the Sacraments had been unknown for years. Their cruel and violent lives had hardened their hearts, but the very appearance of Catherine seemed to bring with it an atmosphere of charity. It was not long before her influ-

ence brought about the longed-for reconcilia-
tion. The neighboring lords and chieftains came
under the spell and at Catherine's prayer were
ready to lay aside their quarrels and to make
peace with their enemies.

Every day brought some fresh work to do for
God, and so it came to pass that Catherine's
visit at Rocca d'Orcia lengthened from days into
months. Countess Bianchina would gladly have
kept both Catherine and her companions forever, such was the love and admiration in which
she held her, and the country people, hearing
of the presence of the *Beata Popolana* in their
midst, came flocking to the castle.

Not only did they bring with them their sick,
but even people possessed by devils, for they had
heard of the wonderful cures effected by Catherine's prayers, or even the touch of her hand.
Francesco Malevolti, one of the young noblemen who was with Catherine at Rocca d'Orcia,
has left us an account of the scenes which took
place in his presence.

One day twelve peasants appeared carrying an
unfortunate man bound with ropes and with
heavy shackles on his hands and feet. He was a
demoniac, they said, who had already injured
several persons in a fearful manner, biting and
tearing with his teeth all who approached him.
They had consented to carry him to Rocca d'Or-

cia on condition that he was very securely bound, but they had had an extremely difficult task to get him there. Indeed, the man, whom they had laid down in the courtyard, was screaming and roaring in a manner that seemed hardly human, glaring and trying to bite those who came near him, like a wild beast. Word was brought to the Countess Bianchina, who asked Catherine if she would come with her to the courtyard, without telling her the reason, for she was always very reluctant to meddle with such cases. At first she resisted, but overcome at last by the entreaties of the Countess, she went to the courtyard, followed by most of the household.

At the sight of her the demoniac uttered such terrible cries and struggled so furiously in his bonds that all were afraid; but Catherine, turning to the Countess, asked her: "What has this poor man done that he should be so cruelly bound? For the love of God bid them set him free; do you not see how he is suffering?"

Then turning to the men: "Dearest brothers," she said, "do not leave this creature of God in such pain; loose him and give him some refreshment. There is nothing the matter with him." "Lady," they replied, "he has injured several of our people fearfully; still, if you will promise to remain near us we will set him free at your command." Then Catherine came close to the poor creature and bade them loose him in the name of Jesus Christ: at which words he lay quite still and let the men handle him without moving.

"Now," said Catherine, "lift him up, he is very weak and needs refreshment. You will see that when he has had some food he will be no longer the same man." No sooner was the demoniac set on his feet than he came humbly and knelt down before Catherine, who blessed him with the Sign of the Cross. He remembered nothing of what had passed and was very much astonished to find himself at Rocca d'Orcia instead of in his own village, not knowing how he had gotten there. They gave him something to eat, after which he left the castle in perfect health with those who had brought him and was never troubled in the same way again.

Don Francesco tells us of several other cases of the same kind which were brought to Catherine and which were cured in the presence of Countess Bianchina, Fra Santi, Fra Raimondo and several others, besides the members of the household.

The fame of the *Beata Popolana* spread far and wide. The people came pouring into the castle to see and hear her. Men and women who had not been to the Sacraments for thirty or forty years and whose lives had been spent in the contempt of God's laws were seized at the very sight of her with sorrow for their sins. Fra Raimondo and the other friars were kept all day in the confessionals, so that they had scarcely time to take food; but Catherine's joy was so great that they forgot their weariness to exult with her over the harvest that was being gathered for God. The news of what was passing even reached Gregory XI in Rome, who granted special powers to Fra Raimondo and his colleagues and sent others to help them in their ministry.

While all this was going on at Rocca d'Orcia, Monna Lapa and the others who had been left behind at Siena were crying out at Catherine's long absence.

"Dearest Mother," she wrote, in answer to a piteous complaint from Monna Lapa, "your miserable child is in this world for one thing, and that is to do the will of her Creator. I do beg of you, if I remain here longer than you like, do not be vexed . . . I am persuaded that if you knew the whole business you would be the first to tell me to remain."

The governors of Siena then took it into their heads to imagine that Catherine and Fra Raimondo were plotting with the Salimbeni against the republic and wrote desiring her instant return. She had some difficulty in persuading them that they were mistaken.

"We are only plotting to defeat the devil," she writes, "and to deprive him of the lordship that he has assumed over man by mortal sin, and to take hate from man's heart and pacify him with Christ Crucified and with his neighbor. These are the plots that we are weaving."

But these contradictions were nothing to what was to follow. The Pope, having heard much of Fra Raimondo's wisdom and holiness, summoned him to Rome to make him Prior of the Minerva—the head church of the Dominicans.

Fra Raimondo had been Catherine's confessor for years, as well as her most devoted friend. No one understood her or helped her as he did, associated with her, as he had been, in all the most wonderful events of her life. But God asked, and she gave with a brave heart. They were to meet again but once in this world. "The suffering I have experienced," she wrote to Alessia, who shared all her secrets, "has reminded me of my want of virtue and made me know my own imperfection. Rejoice then on the Cross with me, for the Cross is the bed and the table of the soul whereon she rests and takes her food, even the fruit of patience, in peace and repose."

Fra Raimondo's journey to Rome was to bear directly on Catherine's life. On his way he stayed for a short time in Florence, where he was assured by one of the rulers that the people as a whole desired peace with the Pope and that the war was only kept up by a small party in the State to suit their own interests. He mentioned this to Gregory when he reached Rome, and a few days after, as they were talking together, the Pope said suddenly: "I believe that, if Catherine were to go to Florence, peace might be secured." The whole matter was arranged within a few days. The refusal of the Florentines to come to terms was a great distress to the Pope, whose health was failing fast.

"May God give him grace to be courageous and never to turn back on account of any difficulty," wrote Catherine to Fra Raimondo; "may he be firm and constant, not fearing labor, hungering only for God and for souls and not troubling himself about temporal losses. Dear Father," she adds, "stand by His Holiness and be full of courage; do all you can for God and for souls until death."

She set out for Florence shortly afterward with her mother, Stefano Maconi and several other companions.

The interdict, the most terrible punishment that could afflict a rebellious people, had now lasted for seventeen months. The city groaned under the burden, and the government, fearing that the growing discontent of the Florentines would force them to submit to the Holy See, had issued a decree ordering priests to disregard the Pope's authority and to administer the Sacraments as before. All who were loyal churchmen left Florence; those who preferred to submit to the rulers of the Republic remained and obeyed their decree.

The first thing to be done was to put a stop to this open violation of the Pope's commands. Catherine assembled the members of the government and addressed them three times with such convincing eloquence that they agreed to observe the interdict. Stefano Maconi has described for us the scene where one frail woman, quietly facing the leaders of a revolution, by sheer force of holiness bent them to her will.

The question of peace had now to be considered. We have already seen that there were two parties in the State: one for peace and one for war. The latter, who thought only of their own private interests, were not likely to be moved by Catherine's arguments. Even the members of the peace party quarreled among themselves and would not take her advice. The people began to murmur, and the war party, taking advantage of the growing discontent, told them that Catherine was the cause of all the disturbance.

The mob at last broke loose, burning and sacking the houses of several of the rulers, and breaking into the prison, set free the criminals, who joined their ranks. Goaded on by the members of the war party and reinforced by all the ruffians in the town, they set out in search of Catherine, who had taken refuge in a garden, shouting, "Let us take that wicked woman and burn her or cut her in pieces."

The shouts and cries came nearer and nearer, and still Catherine prayed on peacefully, surrounded by her people. When the savage mob burst into the garden, she went quietly to meet them and knelt humbly at the feet of the foremost ruffian, who was brandishing a sword.

"I am Catherine," she said; "do to me what you will, but do not touch my companions." At these words the man's courage seemed to fail him: "Flee," he cried, "flee!"

"I am very well where I am," replied Catherine; "where would you have me go? If you mean to kill me, do so. I shall not resist."

At this the man turned with all his companions and left the garden. The danger was over and all rejoiced. Catherine alone was sad, for she would have been glad to give her life for Christ's Church.

The terror in the city was so great that no one dared to receive her, but she had declared that she would not leave Florence until peace was made. She retired with her companions to a solitary place outside the town but within the bounds of the city. The riots still continued.

In the meantime Gregory XI died and Urban VI was elected Pope. Catherine at once wrote to him on behalf of "the sheep who are out of the sheepfold. Let Your Holiness triumph over their hardness of heart," she continues, "and have pity on the souls that perish. Do with me what you like, only grant me the favor I ask of you, miserable as I am."

The rulers were growing anxious, for the city was in a ferment. In the beginning of July 1378 the terms of peace were finally settled. A messenger from Rome rode through the gates carrying a branch of olive in his hand according to the custom of the time. Catherine, writing in her joy to her disciples at Siena, sent a few leaves from the precious bough that meant so much to Florence.

"O dearest children," she writes, "God has heard the cry . . . of His servants . . . And even as persons who now begin to see, they say: Thanks be to Thee, O Lord, Who hast reconciled us with our Holy Father . . . Rejoice, exult in Christ sweet Jesus . . . Now is made the peace, in spite of those who would have prevented it."

Chapter 8

THE SEED OF SORROW

"I turn me and lean against the most Holy Cross of Christ Crucified, and there I will fasten me." —*Letters of St. Catherine*

ON the death of Gregory XI, the Cardinals were resolved to elect a Frenchman as Pope. The papal court would then return to Avignon and take up the old easy life with its luxurious surroundings. The Romans, on the other hand, were determined that Gregory's successor should be an Italian, and they lost no time in letting their intentions be known.

During the conclave that was to decide the question, a huge crowd gathered round the Vatican shouting, "Give us a Roman or at least an Italian Pope!" An embassy consisting of the most eminent men in the city waited upon the Cardinals to warn them of the popular feeling. During the night there were riots in the streets and the state of affairs looked somewhat threatening.

The French Cardinals, who could not agree

as to their candidate, thought it better under
the circumstances to elect an Italian. Their choice
fell upon the Archbishop of Bari, a Neapolitan,
a man whose honesty and purity of life caused
him to be universally respected. The election
took place amid a great turmoil, but there is no
doubt that the Cardinals themselves considered
it valid.

On Easter Day the new Pope, who had taken
the name of Urban VI, was crowned, and the
Sacred College, having made known the result
of the conclave to the sovereigns of Europe and
to the six French Cardinals who had remained
at Avignon, made their act of homage to the
new Pontiff. Urban was known to all as a man
of austere life, zealous for the glory of God and
the good of the Church. Those who knew him
well were aware that he had a harsh and severe
temper, but they were scarcely prepared for what
was to follow.

The new Pope set about the difficult work of
reform with a violence and a want of tact that
destroyed all the good he was earnestly trying
to do. He rebuked the Cardinals in such unmea-
sured language for the lives they led and the
splendor of their households that they could
scarcely contain their anger. He seemed indeed
to have the unfortunate gift of offending everybody. Queen Joanna of Naples, who had even

sent Otho of Brunswick, her own husband, to Rome to offer her congratulations to the Pope, was so indignant at the way in which he was received that she, who might have been Urban's most powerful friend, became his bitterest enemy.

Catherine learned something of what was going on in Rome from Fra Raimondo. "Act with benevolence and a tranquil heart," she wrote to Urban, whom she had known at Avignon; "for the love of Jesus, restrain those too quick movements with which nature inspires you. God has given you a great heart; I beg of you to act so that it may become great supernaturally, and that full of zeal for virtue and the reform of Holy Church, you may also acquire a manly heart, founded in true humility."

Unfortunately Urban did not take her advice. One by one the French Cardinals withdrew to Anagni, followed by many prelates and officials of the papal court. They began to circulate reports that Urban's election had not been lawful; they had been forced to make him Pope, they declared, on account of the threats of the Romans. Catherine wrote to two of them of whom she had hoped better things.

"I hear," she says, "that discord has broken out between Christ on earth and his followers . . . I solemnly entreat you by the Precious Blood that has redeemed you, do not separate from your Head . . . Alas, what misery! All the rest seems but a straw, a mere shadow, compared to the danger of schism."

The danger, alas, had become a reality. The Cardinals had written to Urban commanding him to lay down his usurped dignity and, on his refusal, had proclaimed Cardinal Robert of Geneva, the cruel and bloodthirsty leader of the papal troops in Italy, as Pope under the title of Clement VII. The French King and Joanna of Naples at once acknowledged him, while many of the other nations found it hard to decide whether Urban or Clement was the rightful Pope. Richard II of England remained faithful to Urban, while the King of Scotland, David II, always a firm ally of the French, decided for Clement.

The news went near to breaking Catherine's heart. "I hear," she writes to Urban, "that those incarnate demons have elected an Anti-Christ, whom they have exalted against you, the Christ on earth, for I confess and deny not that you are the Vicar of Christ."

The great schism that was to last for forty years, to the desolation of all Christendom, had begun. With a fearless hand Catherine tore away the veils behind which the baseness of the Cardinals had been concealed from the eyes of the world.

"You have deserted the light," she writes to them, "and gone into darkness; the truth, and joined you to a lie . . . I know what moves you . . . your self-love, which can brook no correction. . . . For before he began to bite you with words and wished to draw the thorns out of the sweet garden, you confessed and announced to us that Pope Urban VI was true Pope. . . . This last fruit that you bear which brings forth death, shows what kind of trees you are and that your tree is planted in the earth of pride, which springs from the self-love that robs you of the light of reason."

Urban's position was a most difficult one. Left alone in Rome, deserted by all the Cardinals save one who remained only to die, he had created others to fill the vacant places, but he was surrounded by enemies.

The castle of St. Angelo was in the hands of French captains who refused to give it up; the ships of Clement lay in the Tiber, while Joanna of Naples was gathering troops to march on Rome.

Fra Raimondo of Capua, standing loyally by Urban, doubtless spoke often to him of Catherine and her efforts in his behalf. The Pope, remembering how at Avignon he had been struck by her wisdom and virtue, bade Fra Raimondo write bidding her in the name of holy obedience to come to Rome without delay.

Once more therefore she left Siena and, with the usual little band of companions, made her way to the Eternal City, which she was never more to leave. Stefano Maconi remained behind at Siena, and it is from his correspondence with the family that we know much that happened during the stirring days that followed.

The Pope received Catherine in a public audience immediately after her arrival and asked her to address the new Cardinals. She spoke to them in burning words of their duty to Christ and His Vicar, exhorting them to have confidence and faith, to do God's work and fear nothing.

"This little woman puts us all to shame by her courage," said Urban when she had finished. "What need the Vicar of Christ fear, although the whole world stand against him? Is not Christ more powerful than the world? And He can never abandon His Church."

She tried to impress on the Pope that he must seek to conquer his enemies by patience and charity. Though wholly in sympathy with his courage and zeal for reform, she could not fail to regret the violent temper that went so far to spoil all he undertook. But Urban was not an easy man to guide, and Catherine with gentle tact hit on a plan to make her advice acceptable.

It was about Christmas time, and with her own hands, skilled in all housewifely labors, she prepared for the Pope a little present of oranges preserved in sugar and gilded. A letter accompanied the gift, in which, after expressing her great grief for the sorrows that were weighing so heavily on his heart, she writes: "That fruit (of suffering) seems bitter when first we taste it, but when the soul is resolved to suffer until death for Jesus Crucified, it becomes truly sweet." A little description of the process by which the oranges had been preserved follows.

"So it is with the soul that loves virtue," she continues. "The beginnings are bitter . . . but the waters of grace will draw out the bitterness . . . and it is filled with the strength of perseverance while it is preserved in the honey of patience mingled with humility. Then when the fruit is finished and prepared, it is gilded outside with the gold of an ardent charity . . . (which) appears in the patience with which the soul serves its neighbor, bearing him with great tenderness and steeping us in that sweet bitterness which we cannot but feel when we see God offended and souls perishing."

The much-needed lesson could scarcely have been more delicately given. If anyone could have tamed the rough and violent Pontiff it would have been Catherine, and in her presence he seems to have been gentler than was his wont.

She desired that he should surround himself with true and devoted servants of God, and it was at her suggestion that he wrote summoning to Rome several of her disciples in Siena, among them the Prior of Gorgona and the hermits of the wood of Lecceto. To her great astonishment, not to say disgust, some of them refused to leave their peaceful retreat to plunge into the turmoil of Rome. Catherine wrote to them in vigorous remonstrance: "If you would do any good, it will not do for you to stand still and to say, 'I shall lose my peace . . .' Follow the call of God and of His Vicar . . . quit your solitude and run to the field of battle."

A second letter followed the first, which seemed to have failed in its effect.

"This is the time for all true servants of God to show their fidelity and for us to see the difference between those who love God for Himself and those who only love Him for their own consolation . . . It seems from the letter which Fr. William has sent me that neither he nor you intend to come. Fr. Andrea of Lucca and Fr. Paulinus have not acted so; they are old and infirm, but they set out at once."

Since the days of her correspondence with the Queen of Naples on the subject of the Crusade, Catherine had followed the career of that most amazing woman with grief and many prayers. Joanna was now devoting herself heart and soul to the cause of the anti-Pope, and when Urban suggested to Catherine that she should go in company with St. Catherine of Sweden, at that time a nun in Rome, to try to win her over to the cause of the Church, she caught eagerly at the idea.

Fra Raimondo was sent to talk the matter over with St. Catherine of Sweden. She was a daughter of the great St. Bridget and had known Joanna well of old, too well to be able to hold out any hopes of success. Fra Raimondo, who believed the Queen of Naples to be capable of any crime, feared to trust two defenseless women to her mercy and persuaded the Pope to give up the project. Catherine was greatly disappointed. She had hoped to win Joanna for Christ, and Fra Raimondo's prudence did not commend itself to her at all.

"If Agnes and Margaret and so many other holy virgins had made all these reasonings," she said, "they would never have won the martyr's crown."

Perhaps the only man who could now have checked the schism was Charles V of France. The Cardinals who had caused it were Frenchmen, and their chief aim was the return of the popes to Avignon. They had urged on the King the advantages of this arrangement to himself, but he was still hesitating and not yet entirely committed to Clement's cause. Urban believed that if a trustworthy ambassador could be found who would undertake to set the true facts of the case before him, he might yet be gained. No one could be fitter for such a task, the Pope told himself, than Fra Raimondo, who had been in Rome at the time of the election and whose wisdom was equal to his holiness.

In spite of her grief at the thought of losing him so soon again, Catherine was the first to urge him to go. Before he left Rome they had one last talk together. "Now, go where God calls you," she said when it was ended. "I think that in this life we shall never again speak together as we have done just now."

It was perhaps because she knew the truth of her words that Catherine went with Fra Raimondo down to the Tiber, where the boat lay in readiness that was to take him on his journey. As it pushed out from the shore, she knelt and, weeping, made the Sign of the Cross over the beloved friend and father whom she was never to see in this life again. It was a difficult and dangerous mission, and her heart longed to share the peril. She dispatched a letter to meet the travelers at Pisa. "We must declare the truth," she says bravely, "and not keep silence out of fear, but be ready generously to give our life for Holy Church."

To Catherine, Rome was above all things the city of the Church Triumphant. The noble army of martyrs overshadowed it with their presence; the very ways she trod were hallowed by their footsteps and washed by their blood. To her the Colosseum was ever thronged with an invisible cloud of witnesses, men and women, aye, and children too, who had counted the world and all that was in it as loss that they might win Christ. Torn by the teeth of beasts or hacked in pieces by the weapons of the Roman soldiers, they had passed through the bitter anguish of the moment to the joy which is eternal—from hope to vision.

A beautiful story is told of St. Gregory the Great, how that when ambassadors of the Emperor Mauritius came to Rome asking for relics of the martyrs, he bade one who was standing by take them to the Colosseum and give them a handful of sand from the arena. This was not what they had expected, and they complained to the Pope—who, taking the sand in his hand pressed it gently, and lo! drops of fresh blood oozed through his fingers. "The sand of the Colosseum," he said reverently, "is soaked with the blood of the martyrs."

Chapter 9

AGAINST THE TIDE

"It is not the hour to seek one's self for one's self, nor to flee pains in order to possess consolations; nay, it is the hour to lose one's self." —*Letters of St. Catherine*

IT was duty alone that had drawn Fra Raimondo from a humble life of prayer and penance in his quiet cell in the Minerva to act as papal envoy to the King of France. Catherine's trumpet tones were ringing in his ears; she was bidding him go forth and die, if need be, for the rightful cause, to glory in suffering and in toil and to conquer in the name of Christ. By nature he was neither a soldier nor a diplomat, but a man of deep wisdom and insight into spiritual things—a man of thought rather than of action.

The ship in which he had embarked, having escaped the galleys of Clement, which were still guarding the mouth of the Tiber, reached Pisa in safety. From thence the travellers went by sea to Genoa, where they landed and proceeded on their way to France. At the frontier Jacopo di Ceva, Fra Raimondo's companion, was seized by the soldiers of Clement, and he himself was warned that his arrival had been expected and that he would meet with certain death were he to continue his journey. He therefore returned to Genoa, where he wrote to Urban telling him of what had taken place and remained awaiting further orders.

To the Pope his conduct seemed perfectly reasonable; he bade Fra Raimondo stay where he was for the present and do his best to spread the truth among the Genoese. On Catherine, however, the news fell like a blow. She could not understand how anyone could fail to share her thirst for martyrdom, more especially one who was so wholly in sympathy with her on all points as Fra Raimondo. She expected heroism from those she loved, and in her eyes, at least, he had not behaved like a hero.

"You were not worthy to stay in the field of battle," she wrote to him, "but were driven back like a child; and you fled away willingly and were glad at the grace that God granted to your weakness . . . how blessed would your soul and mine have been if with your blood you had built up a stone in Holy Church for love of the Blood."

From a letter which followed later it is evi-

dent that although Fra Raimondo feared that
Catherine might love and respect him the less
for his lack of ardor in seeking the martyr's
crown, he had no doubt but that she would be
glad that he had escaped with his life.

"I beg you, dearest Father," she writes, "to
pray earnestly that you and I both together may
drown ourselves in the Blood of the humble
Lamb, which will make us strong and faithful
. . . You did not seem to yourself strong enough
for me to measure you with my measure, and
on this account you were in doubt lest my affection and love to you were diminished . . . Could
you ever believe that I wished anything else than
the life of your soul? Had you been faithful, you
would not have gone about vacillating so, nor
fallen into fear toward God and toward me; but
like a faithful son, ready for obedience, you
would have gone and done what you could. And
if you could not have gone upright, you would
have gone crawling . . . This faithful obedience
would have accomplished more in the sight of
God and in the hearts of man than all human
prudences. My sins have prevented me from seeing it in you . . . I, a vile slave, who am placed
in the Field where blood was shed for love of
Blood (and you have left me here, and gone
away with God), shall never pause from working for you."

This was not the only grief that touched Catherine through those who were dear to her. Stefano Maconi, the best beloved of her disciples, had been left behind on account of family affairs in Siena, from whence he kept up a lively correspondence with the "family" in Rome. Catherine, and Catherine alone, knew all that underlay Stefano's merry and light-hearted exterior. He had received a call to the religious life, and for some time past, nature and grace had been pulling in opposite directions. He was restless and uneasy in that world of which he was the spoiled child and in which with all his gifts he seemed destined to shine. Reading between the lines in the letters that seemed so full of life and gaiety Catherine had discerned the struggle that was going on, and she wrote bidding him come to Rome. But she had scarcely finished writing when a letter was put into her hands from the Abbot of Monte Oliveto, telling her that Stefano was about to join his community.

Although Catherine was glad for the young man's own sake, the thought that he, who had been used to give her all his confidence and seek her help and counsel in every event of his life, had come to this decision without a word to her, and had even let her learn the news from another, was a cruel blow to her loving and sensitive heart.

And after all, it was only a misconception.

The abbot had misunderstood Stefano completely. He was busy at the moment trying to settle the family affairs that kept him in Siena, that he might hasten to his beloved Mother, for he had heard that the others were beginning to be anxious about her health. She alone, as he well knew, had the key to his heart and was therefore the only one who could help him.

The conduct of Joanna of Naples, for whose conversion Catherine still hoped, was an additional grief to her. In April 1379 the papal forces, assisted by the Roman citizens, had gained a complete victory over the army of Clement, who had invaded the Roman territory. The French in consequence had been obliged to surrender the fortress of Sant' Angelo, which had been in their hands since the departure of the Cardinals for Anagni.

The victory was believed by the Romans to be due to Catherine's prayers, and Urban, at her suggestion, resolved to make a solemn act of thanksgiving to God. Walking barefoot and attended by an immense number of clergy and laity, he went in procession through the city to St. Peter's amid the enthusiastic devotion of the people.

On the defeat of his troops Clement had fled in terror to Naples, where Joanna received him with royal pomp and paid him homage with all her court, a court which had the name of being one of the worst in Europe.

The Neapolitans, however, were far from sharing the opinions of their Queen. Urban was their countryman and they were for him to a man. The homage paid to the anti-Pope filled them with horror and indignation. They assembled in crowds, shouting: "Long live Pope Urban!" and soon broke into open rebellion. In a few days the city was in their hands, and Clement was again obliged to flee. With some difficulty he reached Gaeta, from whence he got safely back to Avignon.

Civil war was now raging in Naples, and Joanna did not know where to look for help. In order to pacify her people she announced that she had deserted the cause of Clement, and ambassadors were dispatched to Rome to make her peace with Urban.

Catherine rejoiced to think that Joanna had at last been forced to see the error of her ways, but her joy was short-lived. The submission had been only a trick to gain time while her husband was gathering a body of German troops to put down the insurrection. As soon as this had been successfully done, Joanna threw off the mask. Her ambassadors were recalled from Rome, and she announced herself once more as the partisan of Clement.

Catherine made one last attempt to save the unhappy queen from the fate that she seemed determined to bring upon herself by sending her a letter which could have scarcely failed to touch a heart less hardened than Joanna's.

"Dearest Mother in Christ sweet Jesus," she begins, "I, Catherine, servant and slave of the servants of Jesus Christ, write to you in His Precious Blood, with desire to see you compassionate to your own soul and body . . . Oh, how blessed my soul would be could I come into your parts, and lay down my life to restore to you the good of Heaven, and the good of earth . . . Do not await the time which you are not sure of having. Do not choose that my eyes should have to shed rivers of tears over your wretched soul and body—a soul which I hold as my own . . . Fear, fear God, and place Him before your eyes, and think that God sees you, and His justice wills that every fault be punished and every good rewarded. Be merciful, ah, be merciful to yourself."

But the moment of grace was past—Joanna had made her choice deliberately. She had turned her back on that better self which Catherine's earlier letters seemed to have awakened into life for a moment, and she held on her downward way. Joanna was excommunicated by Urban some

time after on the discovery of a plot to assassi-
nate him which she had set afoot, and she died
a violent death in the very castle where she was
said to have caused her first husband to be
murdered.

The rejoicings that followed on the victory of
the papal troops did not last for long. The
Romans were proud and easily offended, and
Urban was not the most conciliatory of men.
The Prefect of Rome, who was neither a loyal
churchman nor a law-abiding man, had taken
possession of Viterbo, and Urban was determined
to dislodge him at any cost.

It was an unfortunate moment to choose to
quarrel with a powerful enemy, and Catherine
begged the Pope to be prudent. She wrote urging him to call a council general of the chief
citizens, if need be, to decide the matter; to listen to their advice and, above all, to proceed
with gentleness and moderation. "You know the
character of your Roman children," she says,
"that it is easier to lead them by gentleness than
by any other force or by harsh words. And you
know that it is most necessary for you and for
the Church just now to keep the people loyal
and obedient to Your Holiness. Pardon me, sweetest and holiest Father, for saying these things to
you. I trust that your humility and kindness is
content that they should be said to you."

But it was difficult, if not impossible, for Urban to conciliate his enemies. The Romans at last broke into open revolt and even threatened to take his life. Nothing remained to Catherine but to pray and to suffer. She besought God to prevent the people from carrying out their threats. To her the city seemed full of devils, urging men on to evil. The fires of suffering were wasting her frail body as she wrestled with the justice of God, offering herself to suffer and to die for her people and for Holy Church. She was tormented by evil spirits who raged against her unceasingly, crying out that she had always pursued them and that they would be revenged on her. Still the prayer of intercession went up to Heaven, only interrupted by her efforts to pacify the leaders of the revolt.

At last the people armed themselves and marched on the Vatican. Urban, who, if lacking in tact, was certainly not lacking in courage, robed himself in his pontifical vestments, ordered the gates of the palace to be thrown open and awaited them calmly, seated on the papal throne. At the sight of the quiet dignity of Christ's Vicar, the crowds fell back and left the palace without doing any harm.

Peace was at last made, a peace which the Romans attributed to the prayers of Catherine and her influence over the revolutionary leaders. It was the last act in her political life. Her work, outwardly at least, was at an end.

Chapter 10

FROM CROSS TO CROWN

"O Eternal God, receive the sacrifice of my life in this Mystical Body of Holy Church. I have naught to give save what Thou hast given me." —*Prayer of St. Catherine*

THE last months in Rome had been a time of intense suffering for Catherine both in soul and body; she had labored incessantly in the cause of Christ, bearing sorrow after sorrow with a breaking heart. The mysterious agony that was to last for three months had already begun, and to those who watched her with loving eyes it seemed as if she were suffering in a spiritual manner that martyrdom which she had always so ardently desired.

Early in February Barduccio Carrigiani wrote to his sister, a nun in Florence: "I think you know that her prayers were of such intensity that one hour of prayer more consumed that poor little body than two days upon the rack would have done another. Therefore every morning with tears we lifted her up after Communion in such a state that those who so saw her deemed her dead and carried her to her couch. And after an hour or two she would rise up, and we went to San Pietro, and then she set herself to prayer, and she remained there till nearly vespers, after which she returned home so exhausted that she seemed a dead woman, and thus she continued every day . . . until the third Sunday in Lent."

Fra Raimondo was still absent on his ill-starred embassy to France in which a more adventurous man than he might well have failed. His vigorous preaching at Genoa, however, had not been without effect upon the people and had caused considerable annoyance to Clement and his partisans. Catherine wrote two letters of farewell to the beloved friend whom she knew she was never to see again and whose presence would have been so great a consolation. Even then, with her last breath, she urged him to strength and courage in the fight.

"Now is the time, dearest Father, to lose oneself utterly, to think nothing about self, even as did the glorious laborers who with such great love and desire offered up the life of their body and watered this garden with blood, with humble and continual prayers, and by enduring even unto death . . . Now I know not what the Divine Goodness will please to do with me," she continues, after describing her bodily and spiritual suffering. "I do not say that I perceive His Will and intention with regard to me; but as to bodily sensation it seems to me that I am to consume it [her life] at this time with a new martyrdom in the sweetness of my soul, that is, in Holy Church. I have prayed and am praying His infinite mercy to accomplish His Will in me . . .

". . . May that generosity toward the poor and that voluntary poverty which you have always practiced be renewed and refreshed in you with all true and perfect humility. Do not slacken in these for any dignity or exaltation that God may give you, but descend more deeply into that valley of Humility, rejoicing in the table of the Cross."

Then follow a few words of comfort to him in the pain she knows he must be feeling to be so far from her at such a time.

"Do not make yourself unhappy because with bodily presence I am far away from you and you from me; for although your presence would be a very great comfort to me, I have greater consolation and gladness at seeing the fruit that you are producing in Holy Church. Take comfort, take comfort in Christ sweet Jesus, without any bitterness."

On the third Sunday in Lent, as Catherine

was praying in the Church of St. Peter's before Giotto's great picture of the Navicella or "Bark of St. Peter," she had a mysterious vision in which that great ship of the Church which the master had represented was laid upon her shoulders. The weight of it crushed her to the earth, and she understood that in some way she was to give her life as a victim for Holy Church. From that moment her strength seemed to be ebbing gradually away.

Catherine's spiritual family had received a new recruit since she had been in Rome in the person of Tommaso Petra, the secretary of the Pope, who had become her devoted friend and disciple. Hearing of her illness he went to visit her and found her lying on her hard bed of boards, wasted to a shadow. He begged her to give a little word of advice to each of her children that they might treasure in their hearts when she had left them, in order that they might know what she most desired of them. At his request Catherine summoned those of the family who were then in Rome and gave them her last instructions.

"Let them practice continual and humble prayer," she said, "and refrain from judging others or even discussing their doings. Let them put their trust and confidence in God, and love one another, that they might be truly her beloved children. Let them offer tears and fervent prayers in the sight of God for His Holy Church." Then, having asked their pardon for any pain or trouble she might have caused them, she blessed them one by one in Christ as they knelt weeping by her couch.

On Holy Saturday, Fra Bartolommeo Domenico arrived in Rome. Having heard nothing of Catherine's illness, he was horrified to find such a change in her. She was so weak that she could not raise her voice above a whisper or even turn upon her couch. On Easter Sunday he celebrated Mass in her room. To the amazement of all present, at the moment of Holy Communion she rose and, coming forward with the others, knelt to receive the Blessed Sacrament at his hands. The weakness returned later, but she was able to speak more easily. Fra Bartolommeo was Prior of the Church of St. Dominic at Siena and was forced to return to his monastery a few days afterward, to his great grief, for he would have remained until the end.

Soon after his departure Catherine's prayer was granted, and Stefano Maconi arrived in Rome. He had been told that she was ill and, while praying for her one night in great sorrow, heard a voice calling to him suddenly: "Go to Rome, for the time of thy dear Mother's departure is at hand."

It was beside her deathbed that the light for which he had been waiting so long was at last to break on his soul. God was calling him, Catherine said, to the Carthusian Order, and her words brought great peace to the troubled mind of the young disciple with the consciousness that she had spoken the truth and the desire that God's Will should be done in him.

On the Sunday before Ascension Day, Catherine, whose strength was failing fast, received Extreme Unction. Shortly after it seemed as if the evil spirits were making one more desperate effort to shake the peace of her soul. Then, as if the last battle had been fought and won, her face resumed its expression of radiant joy and she sat up, supported in the arms of Alessia, her beloved daughter and disciple. Fixing her eyes upon the Crucifix, she spoke to her family for the last time of the goodness of God, asking once more their pardon for any pain she might have caused them during her life.

Turning to Monna Lapa, who was crying bitterly beside her, she asked her blessing, but her mother would not be content when she had given it until Catherine had blessed her in return, and she continued to ask her to pray to God that she might not offend Him by her sorrow.

Then Catherine prayed for the Church and for the Pope and for all her friends and children, after which she blessed them all with the Sign of the Cross. "Lord, Thou dost summon me to Thyself," she said, "and I am coming to Thee, not by my own merits, but solely through Thy mercy, which mercy I crave from Thee in virtue of Thy Blood."

"Then sweetly, with her face like an Angel's," says Barduccio, "bowing down her head she gave up the ghost."

Thus on April the 29th, the Sunday before Ascension Day, in the year 1380, Catherine, the blessed Spouse of Christ, passed joyfully to her eternal rest. Her three and thirty years of labor and suffering were over, but the memory of her beautiful life will be fragrant forever in the Church that she loved so well. It was Stefano Maconi who bore the body of his beloved friend and Mother to the Church of the Minerva, where it was exposed, clad in the familiar white robe and black mantle, to the veneration of the people.

Men and women thronged to kiss the feet or to touch the garments of the Saint, bringing with them friends and relations, infirm either in body or in soul, to be recommended to her prayers. The noise of the miracles that were worked spread so rapidly through the city that the church was crowded with people both by day and night. Stefano and the other disciples watched beside the body until the funeral, at which Pope Urban himself had commanded all the clergy in Rome to be present. A solemn Requiem was sung two days later at the request of the Roman citizens, in gratitude to the friend who had labored so earnestly for their welfare.

At the time of Catherine's death Fra Raimondo was purposing to leave Genoa for Pisa. He was anxious about the journey that lay before him, for a storm was raging on the sea and the soldiers of Clement were lying in wait to take vengeance on him for the crusade he had been preaching against the anti-Pope. He had just said his morning Mass and was going to make his first preparations for departure when he stopped to say the *Regina Coeli* before the statue of the Madonna. Suddenly a voice spoke in his heart: "Fear not, fear not," it said, "I am here for your sake; I am in Heaven for you. I will protect and defend you." Shortly afterward came the sad news of Catherine's death, and Fra Raimondo understood.

To Tommaso Petra it was also given to share in the knowledge of Catherine's joy. He saw a multitude of heavenly spirits clothed in white who told him that they were accompanying her blessed soul into the presence of Christ. They were followed by the Saint herself walking with downbent head and with her hands full of palm branches. "If it be Catherine," prayed Tommaso, "let me see her face." As he spoke she turned in his direction, smiling at him with the old radiant smile, and went her way to the music of the Angels' song.

Catherine Benincasa had died of a broken heart, yet her soul had been filled even during life with a joy which was not of this world. God had revealed to her that His Bride the Church, "which brings life to man," "holds in herself such life that no man can kill her."

"Sweetest My daughter," He Himself had said to her, "thou seest how she has soiled her face with infirmity and self-love and grown puffed up by the pride and avarice of those who feed at her bosom. But take thy tears and sweats, drawing them from the fountain of My divine charity, and cleanse her face, for I promise thee that her beauty shall not be restored to her by the sword, nor by cruelty nor war, but by peace, and by humble continual prayer, tears and sweats poured forth from the grieving desires of My servants. So thy desire shall be fulfilled in long abiding, and My Providence shall in no wise fail."

If you have enjoyed this book, consider making your next selection from among the following . . .

Prices subject to change.

Saint Michael and the Angels. *Approved Sources* 7.00
Dolorous Passion of Our Lord. *Anne C. Emmerich* 16.50
Our Lady of Fatima's Peace Plan from Heaven. *Booklet* . .75
Three Ways of the Spiritual Life. *Garrigou-Lagrange* . . . 6.00
Mystical Evolution. 2 Vols. *Fr. Arintero, O.P.* 36.00
St. Catherine Labouré of the Mirac. Medal. *Fr. Dirvin* . . 13.50
Manual of Practical Devotion to St. Joseph. *Patrignani* . . 15.00
The Active Catholic. *Fr. Palau* 7.00
Ven. Jacinta Marto of Fatima. *Cirrincione* 2.00
Reign of Christ the King. *Davies* 1.25
St. Teresa of Avila. *William Thomas Walsh* 21.50
Isabella of Spain—The Last Crusader. *Wm. T. Walsh* . . . 20.00
Characters of the Inquisition. *Wm. T. Walsh* 15.00
Philip II. *William Thomas Walsh.* H.B. 37.50
Blood-Drenched Altars—Cath. Comment. Hist. Mexico . . 20.00
Self-Abandonment to Divine Providence. *de Caussade* . . 18.00
Way of the Cross. *Liguorian* 1.00
Way of the Cross. *Franciscan* 1.00
Modern Saints—Their Lives & Faces, Bk. 1. *Ann Ball* . . 18.00
Modern Saints—Their Lives & Faces, Bk. 2. *Ann Ball.* . . 20.00
Divine Favors Granted to St. Joseph. *Pere Binet* 5.00
St. Joseph Cafasso—Priest of the Gallows. *St. J. Bosco* . 5.00
Catechism of the Council of Trent. *McHugh/Callan* 24.00
Why Squander Illness? *Frs. Rumble & Carty* 2.50
Fatima—The Great Sign. *Francis Johnston* 8.00
Heliotropium—Conformity of Human Will to Divine. . . . 13.00
Charity for the Suffering Souls. *Fr. John Nageleisen* . . . 16.50
Devotion to the Sacred Heart of Jesus. *Verheylezoon* . . . 15.00
Sermons on Prayer. *St. Francis de Sales* 4.00
Sermons on Our Lady. *St. Francis de Sales* 10.00
Sermons for Lent. *St. Francis de Sales* 12.00
Fundamentals of Catholic Dogma. *Ott* 21.00
Litany of the Blessed Virgin Mary. (100 cards) 5.00
Who Is Padre Pio? *Radio Replies Press* 2.00
Child's Bible History. *Knecht* 5.00
The Life of Christ. 4 Vols. H.B. *Anne C. Emmerich* 60.00
St. Anthony—The Wonder Worker of Padua. *Stoddard* . . 5.00
The Precious Blood. *Fr. Faber* 13.50
The Holy Shroud & Four Visions. *Fr. O'Connell* 2.00
Clean Love in Courtship. *Fr. Lawrence Lovasik.* 2.50
The Secret of the Rosary. *St. Louis De Montfort* 3.00

At your Bookdealer or direct from the Publisher.
Call Toll Free 1-800-437-5876

Prices subject to change.

ABOUT THE AUTHOR

This book was authored by Mother Frances Alice Monica Forbes, a sister of the Society of the Sacred Heart, Scotland.

The future author was born on March 16, 1869 and was named Alice Forbes. Alice's mother died when she was a child, and her father became the dominant influence in her life, helping to form Alice's virile personality and great capacity for work. She was raised as a Presbyterian.

In 1900 Alice became a Catholic. The Real Presence in the Eucharist had been the big stumbling-block to her conversion, but one day she was hit by the literal truth of Our Lord's words: "This is My Body." Only a few months after her conversion, she entered the Society of the Sacred Heart, becoming a 31-year-old postulant. She seems to have received her vocation at her First Communion, when Our Lord kindled in her heart "the flame of an only love."

In the convent, Sister Forbes used her keen intelligence and strong will to make generously and completely the sacrifices that Our Lord asked of her each day. She put great store by the virtue of obedience. Much of the latter part of her life was spent in illness and suffering, yet she was always kind and uncomplaining—a charming person and a "gallant" soul. Throughout her sufferings the most important thing to her was the love of God. She died in 1936.

Mother Frances Alice Monica Forbes wrote many

books, including a series of interesting short lives of selected Saints called "Standard Bearers of the Faith." One of these books, that on Pope St. Pius X, was very highly regarded by Cardinal Merry del Val, who was a close friend of Pope Pius X.

Other works by Mother Frances Alice Monica Forbes include *St. Ignatius Loyola, St. John Bosco: Friend of Youth, St. Teresa, St. Columba, St. Monica, St. Athanasius, St. Catherine of Siena, St. Benedict, St. Hugh of Lincoln, The Gripfast Series of English Readers* and *The Gripfast Series of History Readers,* various plays, and a number of other books.

The above information is from the book *Mother F. A. Forbes: Religious of the Sacred Heart—Letters and Short Memoir,* by G. L. Sheil (London: The Catholic Book Club, 1948, by arrangement with Longmans, Green & Co., Ltd.).